NATIONAL
GEOGRAPHIC

School Publishing

Weather and Seasons

Cory Phillips

PICTURE CREDITS

Cover, Zefa Images; 1, 2, 4 (left & below right), 5 (above left), 6 (all), 7 (all), 10 (all), 11 (left), 12 (right), 14 (below), 15 (above left), 16 (center right & below left), Photolibrary.com; 4 (above right), 5 (below left, above right & below right), 8 (all), 9 (left), 11 (right), 13 (left), 14 (above right), 16 (above left, center left & below right), Getty Images; 9 (right), 16 (above right), Sarkis Images/Alamy; 12 (above left), 13 (above right), 14 (above left), 15 (above right & below), APL/Corbis.

Produced through the worldwide resources of the National Geographic Society, John M. Fahey, Jr., President and Chief Executive Officer; Gilbert M. Grosvenor, Chairman of the Board; Nina D. Hoffman, Executive Vice President and President, Books and Education Publishing Group.

PREPARED BY NATIONAL GEOGRAPHIC SCHOOL PUBLISHING

Ericka Markman, Senior Vice President and President Children's Books and Education Publishing Group; Steve Mico, Senior Vice President and Publisher; Marianne Hiland, Editorial Director; Lynnette Brent, Executive Editor; Michael Murphy and Barbara Wood, Senior Editors; Bea Jackson, Design Director; David Dumo, Art Director; Margaret Sidlowsky, Illustrations Director; Matt Wascavage, Manager of Publishing Services; Sean Philpotts, Production Manager.

MANUFACTURING AND QUALITY MANAGEMENT

Christopher A. Liedel, Chief Financial Officer; Phillip L. Schlosser, Director; Clifton M. Brown III, Manager.

BOOK DEVELOPMENT

Ibis for Kids Australia Pty Limited.

Published by the National Geographic Society
1145 17th Street, N.W.
Washington, D.C. 20036-4688

ISBN: 0-7922-6051-1

Second Printing June 2006
Printed in China

Contents

Think and Discuss

spring

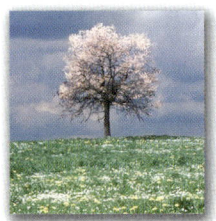

summer

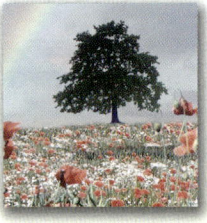

fall

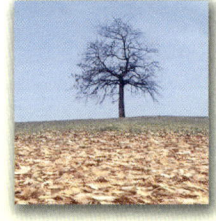

winter

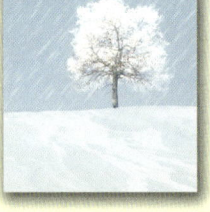

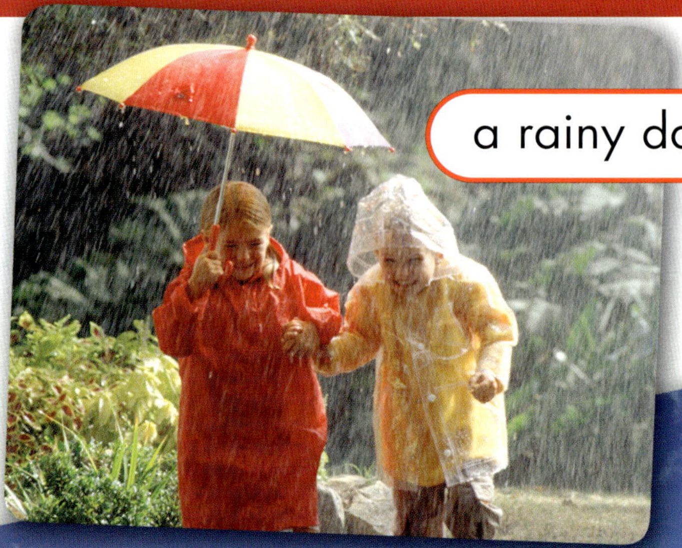
a rainy day

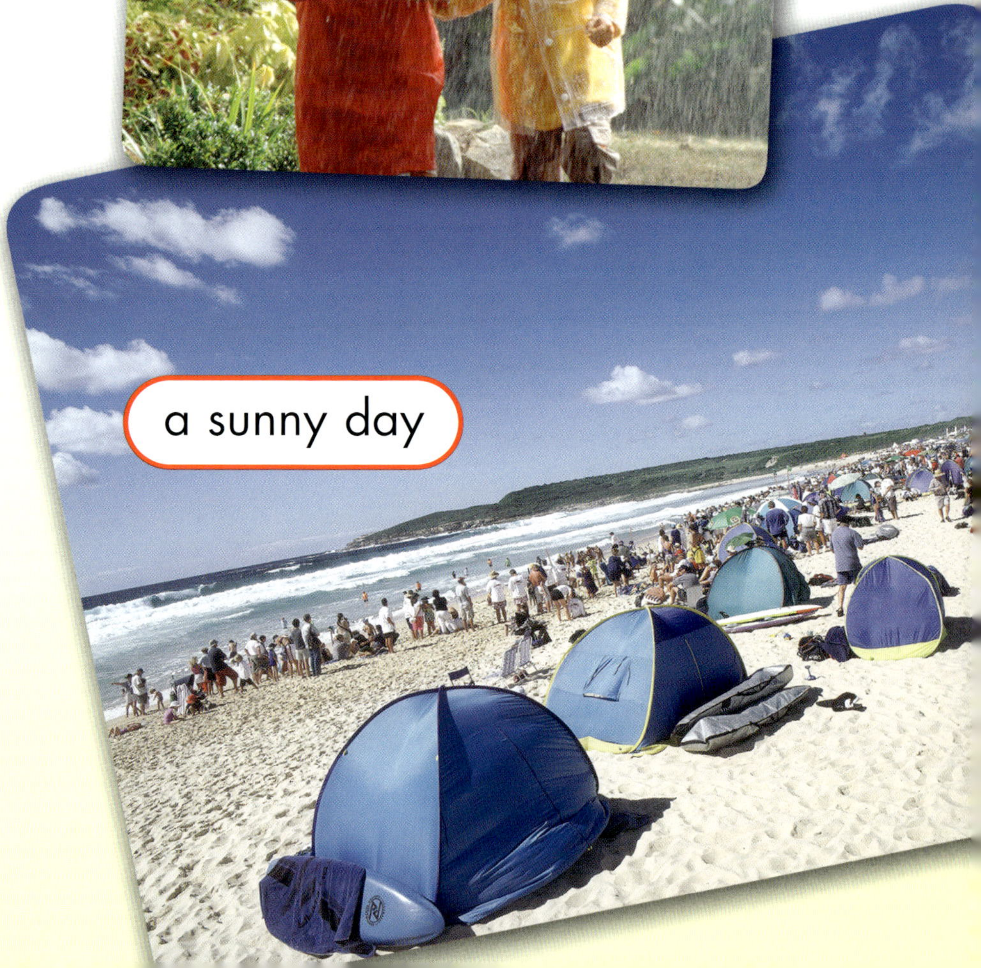
a sunny day

What weather does each photo show? What season could it be?

a snowy day

a windy day

a cloudy day

a stormy day

The Seasons

The weather changes from season to season.

summer

spring

6

fall

winter

The weather changes from day to day, too.

Wind

Sometimes the weather is windy.

 # Rain

Sometimes the weather is rainy.

 # Sun

Sometimes the weather is sunny.

Clouds

Sometimes the weather is cloudy.

❄ Snow

Sometimes the weather is snowy.

Storms

Sometimes the weather is stormy.

14

What is your favorite season?
What is your favorite weather?

spring

summer

fall

winter

cloudy

rainy

snowy

stormy

sunny

windy

Picture Glossary

cloudy

rainy

snowy

stormy

sunny

windy